A History of Britain

TRADE, COLONIZATION AND INDUSTRY

1750–1900

Richard Dargie

FRANKLIN WATTS
LONDON•SYDNEY

First published in 2008 by Franklin Watts

© 2008 Arcturus Publishing Limited

Franklin Watts
338 Euston Road
London NW1 3BH

Franklin Watts Australia
Level 17/207 Kent Street, Sydney, NSW 2000

Produced by Arcturus Publishing Limited,
26/27 Bickels Yard, 151–153 Bermondsey Street, London SE1 3HA

Series concept: Alex Woolf
Editor and picture researcher: Patience Coster
Designer: Phipps Design

Picture credits:
akg-images: 5, 27 (top).
Clipart: 4 (top), 27 (bottom).
Corbis: 6 (Archivo Iconografico/SA), 14 (Bettmann), 15, 16 and cover, 21 (main image).
Dover: 10, 11 (top), 13, 17.
Mary Evans Picture Library: 8, 9, 12 (top, Bruce Castle Museum), 12 (bottom), 19, 22, 23.
The Bridgeman Art Library: 18 and cover (The Stapleton Collection), 20 (The Fleming-Wyfold Art Foundation), 24, 25 (bottom), 26 (bottom) and cover, 29 (top, University of Edinburgh).

Every attempt has been made to clear copyright. Should there be any inadvertent omission, please apply to the publisher for rectification.

A CIP catalogue record for this book is available from the British Library.

Dewey Decimal Classification Number: 941.07

ISBN 978 0 7496 8197 5

Printed in China

Franklin Watts is a division of Hachette Children's Books.

Contents

The Rise of Party Politics

Between 1750 and 1900, Britain became the most important economic power in the world, inventing new industrial technologies that created vast wealth. By 1900 Britain also ruled the largest empire the world had ever seen. However, at the start of the 18th century, this was all to come. Britain was still a largely agricultural society, and political influence rested firmly in the hands of a few powerful men.

The Tory politician Henry Bolingbroke was a Jacobite supporter. When George I came to the throne in 1714, Bolingbroke fled Britain for France, but later returned to continue his career.

Whig and Tory

By 1715, two very different political parties had developed at Parliament. The first party, the Whigs, believed in the rights of Parliament and wanted to limit the powers of the monarch. The second, the Tories, supported the Crown and the Church. Some Tories were rumoured to be secretly loyal to the Stewarts, a factor that kept them out of government from 1714 until 1760. However, while the Whigs governed at Westminster, many Tory landowners held influential posts, such as justices of the peace, throughout the country.

Prime Minister

The new Hanoverian king, George I, spoke little English and was usually content to leave his ministers to govern for him. George II also preferred the Whigs, especially after they voted him an increase of £100,000 in his revenues. Neither king was particularly interested in attending Cabinet meetings, so the day-to-day running of the country ended up in the hands of a first, or 'prime', minister. Sir Robert Walpole never held the title of Prime Minister, but he was in charge of the government from 1721 to 1742.

The Whig politician, Sir Robert Walpole is often said to have been the first 'Prime Minister' of the United Kingdom.

Patronage and 'Corruption'

Walpole controlled hundreds of posts in the armed forces, the Church, and the civil service. Only loyal Whigs who voted for him could expect to get one of these well-paid positions. Of the total number of members of Parliament (MPs) in the House of Commons, about a quarter held minor jobs in government that had generous salaries. Walpole also controlled the election of many MPs. Some represented 'rotten boroughs', where there were so few voters they could all be bribed. These included Old Sarum in Hampshire, an abandoned medieval fort, and Dunwich in Suffolk, an old seaport that had fallen into the sea. There were also 'pocket boroughs', where the main landowner decided who would be the MP. The Duke of Newcastle had fourteen Commons seats 'in his pocket'.

Stable Government

Not all MPs elected by this system were corrupt. For example, the talented William Pitt, who went on to become Prime Minister, was the MP for Old Sarum. The system created stable governments, sometimes with vigorous Tory oppositions, and contributed to the change in British politics during the 18th century. At the start of the century, punishment for a disgraced parliamentarian was likely to be imprisonment; by 1750, he was more likely to be punished by being sacked from his government post.

Rotten Scotland?

Scotland was described as 'one vast rotten burgh'. Many Scottish elections were decided by 'parchment barons'. These were lawyers who held lists of fictitious (made-up) voters that they controlled on behalf of their powerful clients.

Although he was 'elected' to Parliament via the rotten borough of Old Sarum, William Pitt the Elder was an able statesman.

5

Wars for the World

Between 1700 and 1815, Britain fought a series of long wars against France. In conflicts that stretched from Europe to Africa, Asia and the Americas, Britain finally emerged as the world's leading military power.

Marlborough's War

John Churchill, Duke of Marlborough, was an outstanding soldier. In 1704, at Blenheim near Vienna, he inflicted the first major defeat on the French that they had suffered in forty years. He went on to win further battles at Ramillies, Oudenarde and Malplaquet in Belgium. Marlborough's victories secured the first diplomatic triumph of the new kingdom of Great Britain. By the 1713 Treaty of Utrecht, Britain had gained much of French Canada and Gibraltar and the status of a first-rank nation.

The War for the World, 1756-63

By 1756, Britain and France were rivals for trade and territory in India, Africa and North America. The war that began that year therefore was a struggle for world domination. It began badly for Britain. The island of Minorca was lost and the French advanced in Canada. In 1757 however, a tiny British and Indian force under Robert Clive won an astonishing victory at Plassey in Bengal. In 1759, the Royal Navy defeated French fleets in the West Indies and then at

Timeline

1704	• Marlborough wins at Blenheim on the Danube near Vienna
1713	• Britain gains French North America in the Treaty of Utrecht
1757	• Robert Clive defeats the forces of the Nawab of Bengal at Plassey
1759	• The 'Year of Victories' in Canada, the West Indies and India
1763	• Treaty of Paris confirms British supremacy over the French
1805	• Nelson's victory at Trafalgar saves Britain from French invasion
1813	• French forces decisively weakened at the Battle of Leipzig
1815	• Duke of Wellington wins final victory over Napoleon at Waterloo

The Battle of Blenheim, fought on the banks of the River Danube in August 1704, was the Duke of Marlborough's most famous victory.

Quiberon Bay in Brittany, while victories on land followed in Quebec and Germany. The 1763 Treaty of Paris confirmed that Great Britain now controlled an empire that stretched from Canada to the East.

War with Revolutionary France, 1793-1805

In 1789, France underwent a violent revolution and its people were fired with enthusiasm to spread the new ideas of liberty and equality. France's armies seemed unstoppable, sweeping into Holland and forcing the Dutch to abandon their alliance with Britain. In 1796, the charismatic French commander, Napoleon Bonaparte led his army across the Alps. With command of Italy and with Spain as an ally, France controlled the western Mediterranean Sea. French plans to expand into the eastern Mediterranean were only halted by the British Royal Navy, led by Admiral Horatio Nelson, who defeated the French fleet near the mouth of the River Nile in August 1798. The British captured the strategically important island of Malta in 1800 and took control of the Baltic after victory at Copenhagen in 1801.

The Battle of Trafalgar was fought off the Spanish coast in 1805. There the Royal Navy, under Admiral Nelson, defeated a combined French and Spanish force.

Bonaparte

In 1805, the newly crowned Emperor Bonaparte crushed the Austrian and Russian armies at Austerlitz. However, Nelson's destruction of the French fleet at Trafalgar in October gave Britain total command of the seas and dashed Napoleon's plans to invade Britain. In 1809, a British military campaign on the Iberian peninsula (today's Spain and Portugal) sapped French resources that were badly needed elsewhere. After losing over 500,000 men in 1812 in Russia, Napoleon began to run out of troops. With greater resources, Britain and her allies won crushing victories at Leipzig in 1813 and finally at Waterloo in 1815.

More Mouths to Feed

The population of Britain and Ireland rose dramatically after 1750, even though many people emigrated overseas and death rates were high in the squalid areas of towns.

Rising Numbers

The British population increased relentlessly, from ten million in 1750 to twenty-seven million a century later. A far larger number of people were living in cities, and factory towns grew at a rate that astonished people at the time. London grew from 650,000 in 1750 to over two million in 1840. Within one lifetime, the small town of Glasgow in Scotland was transformed, first by the tobacco trade and then by heavy industry, into the Second City of the Empire.

Family Fears

After 1750, thousands of young farm labourers left the land in search of work in the new mills and mines of industrial Britain. Many of them earned high cash wages and were able to marry and raise a family at a younger age than earlier generations. One writer, Thomas Robert Malthus, was worried by this and predicted that the increasing number of mouths would lead to famine by 1850.

Soap and Science

Cheap coal meant it was easier to heat water for bathing, washing clothes and scrubbing homes. Cheap cotton clothes were easy to keep clean, unlike the heavy woollens of earlier times that were seldom washed. Soap and bleach became everyday products. Cleaner, warmer homes were safer places for infants. Not only were more people being born – their chances of surviving into adulthood were far higher. New scientific discoveries helped, particularly the work on vaccination by Edward Jenner, which reduced deaths from smallpox after 1810.

After 1796, Edward Jenner developed a vaccine against smallpox. The illustration of Jenner, below, shows him inoculating his son.

Producing More Food

In 1700 much of Britain was still farmed using traditional methods that produced few surplus crops to sell for cash. In wet years such as the 1690s there was still a chance of famine, and wheat had to be bought in from Europe. However, landowners increasingly changed to new farming methods by enclosing and draining the land, improving the quality of their livestock and growing fodder crops, such as clover and turnips. Farmers were only granted leases if they were willing and able to run their farms efficiently. Thousands of farm labourers lost their land and had to go to the towns in search of a new living.

The Farming 'Craze'

The British public was fascinated by the changes to farming that were producing unimagined quantities of quality food. Thousands joined farming societies to learn about new ideas, such as crop rotation, that improved the condition of soil, or about new machines, such as Jethro Tull's seed drill, that kept young plants apart in neat rows so they could be weeded better.

The old open-field system of farming had allowed the spread of weeds and animal diseases. Enclosing the land with hedges and fences remedied these problems and made land more productive.

Timeline

1750	• Population of Britain and Ireland about ten million
1789	• Andrew Pears first produces his translucent soap
1796	• Edward Jenner tests his theory of vaccination
1798	• Malthus predicts a population disaster
1801	• First official census of the population of Britain
1810	• Domestic bleach produced at St Rollox Chemical Works, Glasgow
1851	• Population of Britain and Ireland over twenty-seven million

Industrial Revolution

After 1750, industrial production in Britain grew at a 'revolutionary' rate. By 1850, Britain was the world's largest trading power.

Water and Steam Power

The first water-powered mill opened in 1771 and was followed by many others, such as Quarry Bank in Cheshire and New Lanark in Scotland. These early factories were built in hilly places next to fast-flowing streams. Change was occurring so fast that the first steam-driven mill was built only nine years later. Steam power had been developed to drain water from coalmines as they went deeper underground. James Watt's improved steam engine was a machine that could be used almost anywhere. By 1870, over 100,000 steam engines were in use throughout Britain, and industry was increasingly concentrated above ground rather than below it.

Coal and Iron

By 1850, over twelve million tons of coal were dug up every year, much of it to fuel British industry. The new deeper mine shafts were difficult to work. After 1815, Davey's safety lamp allowed miners to work in light without igniting firedamp, an explosive mixture of air and methane gas found at depth underground. After 1795, exhaust pumps replaced the 'trappers', children who operated flaps all day to push air to the workers down below. By 1830, steam-powered fans allowed mines to be dug even deeper. In Coalbrookdale in Shropshire, the Darby family of ironmasters perfected the use of coke to smelt iron ore. But this discovery meant that even more coal was needed.

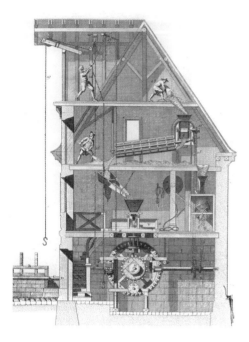

In mills powered by fast-flowing streams and rivers, machines could now be used to speed up all kinds of jobs that once had to be done by hand.

Timeline

1733	• John Kay's 'Flying Shuttle' speeds up the process of weaving
1769	• Richard Arkwright develops the water frame to speed up cotton thread production
1776	• First successful use of Watt's steam engine
1785	• Edmund Cartwright builds the first mechanized power loom
1780-1850	• Golden age of British industry
1815	• Sir Humphrey Davey invents the miners' safety lamp
1851	• Great Exhibition at Crystal Palace in London

Previous ironmasters had used charcoal, even sending shiploads of ore to the Scottish Highlands where trees were plentiful. Now vast industrial enterprises appeared across Britain, such as the Cyfarthfa Works in Merthyr Tydfil, South Wales, and the Carron Iron Works in Falkirk, Scotland.

Early miners worked by candlelight, which meant they were in constant danger of igniting gases trapped underground. The invention of the safety lamp greatly improved miners' working conditions.

Economic Mastery

Thanks to innovative technology and an abundant supply of cheap coal and iron, Britain raced ahead of its European competitors. In the 1820s, British coal production was nine times that of France, Germany and Russia combined. In 1851, more British people lived in towns than in the countryside for the first time. Many of those town dwellers lived in the shadow of a coalmine winding-wheel or a mill chimneystack. Industry was also helped by the 'laissez-faire' attitude of governments who did not want to interfere in industrial matters. As a result, Britain was the 'workshop of the world', a fact celebrated by the Great Exhibition held at Crystal Palace in 1851. Joseph Paxton's purpose-built glass and iron exhibition structure on Sydenham Hill in London housed 13,000 industrial exhibits. This statement of British pride and confidence attracted more than six million visitors from all over Britain.

The Great Exhibition of 1851 showed the extent of Britain's economic and industrial success. It took place at the Crystal Palace, which had been built specially for the occasion in London.

The Transport Revolution

In 1720, the horse was still Britain's most efficient means of transport. By 1850 however, goods and passengers were being transported by way of a vast, new network of canals, roads and railways.

Turnpikes

Around 1700, businessmen began to build fast turnpike, or toll, roads. By 1810 there were 16,000 km (10,000 miles) of turnpike road in Britain and 1,500 daily coach services in and out of London. Inns grew up to provide fresh horses and refreshments for travellers. Newspapers and letters could now be sent quickly and cheaply.

Canals

One of the first managed waterways was the Newry Canal in Ireland, used to move coal from Loch Neagh to market in Dublin. Its success encouraged merchants in Liverpool to fund the Sankey Navigation, a canal built to carry cheap coal to the city. The Duke of Bridgewater's canal also carried coal from his mines at Worsley to Manchester. Onlookers marvelled at the barges on the aqueduct high above the River Irwell, but the real wonder was the canal's effect on the price of coal. It fell by 50 per cent. By 1820, a network of canals had been built wherever manufacturers needed to move heavy materials such as iron ore and clay.

Locomotives

Wooden railways had long been used in coalmines to help horses pull heavy wagons. By 1814, George Stephenson was building steam locomotives that pulled loads of thirty tonnes. In 1825, his *Locomotion* pulled thirty-six wagons containing coal and over 500 passengers at a speed of 24 km/ph (15 mph). The first permanent passenger service was soon in action. In 1830, its first full year of operation, the Liverpool & Manchester Railway carried 445,000 passengers. By the 1840s a railway network had been established, despite the opposition of landowners, canal owners, turnpike trustees, innkeepers and huntsmen who all feared the railways.

A coach passing through a turnpike at night. The term 'pike' referred to the long bar that would block the way until the traveller paid the toll. The toll monies were used to keep the roads in good condition.

A tollgate ticket for roads in south London dating from the turnpike era.

'The Railway King'

The giant of the age was Henry Hudson, who built up a railway empire swallowing up rival companies and merging them into his Midland Railway Company. In 1849 Hudson was accused of corruption. However, the development of the railway system in Britain owed much to the vision, energy and greed of railway speculators like him.

Railway Impact

The railways established one shared national time and provided reliable distribution for all kinds of products such as newspapers and letters. Vegetables and dairy produce were brought to market faster and fresher than in the days of turnpike and canal. Railways also provided people with excursions to seaside towns such as Brighton, Scarborough, Blackpool and Dunoon. By 1875, the wealthy traveller could leave London on an overnight train and take his breakfast in the Highlands of Scotland.

Timeline

1700	• Spread of turnpike, or toll, roads
1757	• Opening of the Sankey Navigation near the River Mersey
1760s	• John Macadam develops his system of drained, cambered roads
1780-1830	• Golden age of coaching on the turnpike road system
1784	• Royal Mail sets up an express postal coach system
1825	• *Locomotion* used to pull coal wagons from Stockton to Darlington
1830	• Liverpool & Manchester Railway opens its passenger service
1840s	• 'Railway Mania' during the great age of railway building

By the 1840s, people of all social classes in all parts of Britain had begun to travel widely by train.

Radical Britain

After the French Revolution, radical ideas spread to Britain but they were suppressed by the authorities, who feared dramatic change.

French Revolution

Many British people welcomed the news of revolution in France in 1789. The radical writer, Thomas Paine believed that the people had the right to change their government if they wished. The British government was so alarmed by Paine's ideas that he was tried for sedition. After 1793, France and Britain were at war and support for Paine's democratic ideas was viewed as treason by the authorities.

Combination Acts

The government knew that many factory workers supported radical ideas and had begun to work together to get higher wages and better conditions. The government's fear of radicalism led to the Combination Acts of 1799 and 1800 that made it illegal for workers to join trade unions.

Working-class Unrest

During the long wars with France the price of bread tripled but the wages of labourers barely rose. With peace in 1815, government supply contracts dried up. Many workers were left unemployed, and at the same time 200,000 ex-servicemen joined the job market. In the midst of this slump, the government passed laws that raised the price of bread again. The unemployed and their families went hungry. Many agreed with the radicals that Parliament should be reformed so that it looked after everyone in Britain and not just the rich.

The demonstration at St Peter's Field in 1819 in Manchester ended in bloodshed, as unarmed protesters were cut down by cavalry troops.

'Peterloo'

As the situation worsened in 1819, a huge meeting was organized at St Peter's Fields in Manchester to demand reform. Fearing a riot, the authorities arrested the main speaker

and sent in the army to make further arrests. Eleven demonstrators were killed and 400 wounded, many by the sabres of the cavalry. This attack on unarmed protesters was nicknamed 'Peterloo'.

Tolpuddle Martyrs

In the 1820s, the Combination Acts were repealed. However, in 1834 the authorities arrested six farm labourers from Tolpuddle in Dorset who had formed a trade union. The men were accused of swearing illegal secret oaths, and sentenced to seven years in prison. Public outrage forced the government to pardon the men, but the damage was done to the trade unions. Despite small victories for the London match girls in 1888 and the dockers in 1889, unions for lower-paid workers had made little progress by 1900.

Co-operatives and the Charter

Working people found other ways to improve their lot. In 1844 in Rochdale, Lancashire, workers set up a co-operative shop selling quality goods at a fair price to its members. The Rochdale shop was a protest against the adulterated foods, such as bread mixed with chalk, that were often sold to working-class people. Other workers joined the Chartists, a group of reformers who drew up petitions demanding the vote for all men, secret ballots,

In 1888, the girls who made matches at the Bryant & May factory in London went on strike. They were protesting against low pay, health hazards and being fined for making mistakes in their work. The fine system was abolished and the strikers were rehired.

Timeline

1791	• Thomas Paine publishes *The Rights of Man*
1819	• Peaceful protesters murdered at 'Peterloo' in Manchester
1824-5	• Repeal of the Combination Acts against trade unions
1834	• Tolpuddle Martyrs condemned for swearing secret oaths
1839	• First Chartist petition for votes for all men rejected by Parliament
1844	• 'Rochdale Pioneers' set up a successful co-operative movement
1848	• Chartist demonstrations in London spark fear of a revolution

Reforming Britain

Between 1833 and 1845, the Whigs and Robert Peel's new Conservative Party passed a number of acts that accepted the government's responsibility for social reform.

Speenhamland

In the 1830s, the reforming Whig government began to tackle ills that had developed in the long years of laissez faire. In much of southern England, labourers received supplements to their wages paid for through the rates (a local tax on property). The system, first applied in the parish of Speenhamland in Berkshire in 1795, only encouraged labourers to have larger families to gain higher payments. It also allowed employers to limit wages.

The Workhouse

After 1834, able-bodied labourers who applied for relief (help from the parish poor fund) had to enter the new workhouses where conditions were made as miserable as possible to deter the lazy. The inmates had to wear a uniform and endure silent meals of thin porridge and hours of hard labour. Throughout the Victorian age, fear of the workhouse encouraged labourers to seek employment rather than apply for relief. With the end of the 'Speenhamland' subsidies, employers were also forced to raise wages.

Workers at a steel mill in Sheffield, South Yorkshire. A series of reform acts led to their working hours being reduced, with half-a-day's holiday on Saturday.

Timeline

1833	• Factory Act begins to improve conditions for child workers in mills
1834	• Poor Law Amendment Act puts many poor people into the workhouses
1835	• New borough councils charged with improving urban conditions
1842	• Mines Act prohibits women and children from working underground
1847	• Working day in factories effectively limited to ten hours
1850	• Factory Act gives mill workers Saturday afternoon off

Factory Acts

In 1833, factory inspectors were appointed to make sure that employers did not hire children younger than nine. The inspectors also ensured that factories followed new regulations on weekly hours of work: forty-eight for children under the age of thirteen and sixty-nine for teenagers. Further laws in 1844 made employers responsible for checking that all machinery was safe to use and giving younger workers time off for education. The working day for all factory workers was reduced to a twelve-hour shift, with one-and-a-half hours' break. Saturday afternoons were also free time.

The Home

Workers needed to be housed close to the mill or mine. This often meant that their accommodation was densely packed and poorly built. Fresh water and drains were seldom provided and piles of filth soon littered the back yards, attracting flies and vermin, while sewage seeped into the water supply. In these conditions, diseases such as bronchitis, tuberculosis, typhoid and cholera were common. Edwin Chadwick's report into the sanitary condition of working-class areas led to the establishment of public health boards in 1848. These worked alongside the reformed borough councils, set up in 1835, to improve the health of 19th-century towns.

The Mines

Some of the worst conditions were endured in the coalmines. Here children as young as four worked alongside their parents, putting in shifts of fourteen hours and learning little of the world above ground. The public was horrified by an 1842 report with its descriptions of the miserable conditions suffered by workers underground. New laws brought in safety measures, restricted children and women to surface jobs, and appointed inspectors to force the changes upon reluctant employers.

Housing like this in London grew up as workers flocked to the cities from the countryside. These slums were often badly built and were breeding grounds for disease.

God's Work

In 18th and 19th-century Britain, religion found its most practical expression in the work of Methodists and Evangelicals, who preached to the urban poor and the 'unbelievers' of distant lands.

Griffith Jones

Many Church of England ministers wanted to help the poor escape their lives of poverty. One of the earliest of these 'Evangelicals' was Griffith Jones, who believed in the power of education. A Welsh clergyman, Jones helped to spread literacy through his 'circulating school' movement. These schools stayed in a location for several months before circulating, or transferring, to the next village.

A vicar preaches to a packed congregation at St Martin's in the Fields church in London. The enthusiasm of the Methodists and Evangelicals was not welcomed by many 18th-century clergymen, who feared they would unsettle society.

Methodists

At Oxford in the 1730s, the brothers John and Charles Wesley were noted for their disciplined approach to Bible study and their distaste for popular amusements. Their regular behaviour earned them the nickname 'Methodists', which they used when they began their missionary activities. George Whitefield had already preached in the open air to the miners of Kingswood near Bristol in 1739. John Wesley followed suit, embarking on a life of mission and travelling hundreds of miles each year on long preaching tours. He preached to the most desperate communities in England, such as the coalminers of the north and the workers from the Cornish tin mines.

Methodist ministers such as John Wesley (pictured) preached to communities the length and breadth of Britain.

Reaction

Local magistrates feared the huge congregations of up to 20,000 working people who gathered to listen to Methodist preachers. Wesley and his colleagues were accused of stirring up social unrest. In time, however, the good work that the Methodists did among the poor – running schools, orphanages and charities – was recognized.

The Missionary Impulse

The Evangelical desire to spread the faith in Africa was connected to the campaign against slavery. British participation in the slave trade was banned in 1807, and slavery was abolished in all British territories in 1833. African chiefs continued in the trade however, to the horror of those like the young David Livingstone, who attended the public lectures of the London Missionary Society. Livingstone began his work in Africa in 1840 with two aims; to spread the Christian message and find new routes across southern and central Africa. He hoped that traders would follow in his footsteps, creating wealth and raising living standards so that no tribe would be forced to sell its children into slavery. There were also missionaries much nearer to home. William Booth's Salvation Army marched in to the poorest areas of Britain's cities to care for the least fortunate.

The Prince of Preachers

Charles Spurgeon was a born preacher whose public speaking 'revived' the faith of thousands. His church had to move to larger halls as his congregation expanded. More than 20,000 listened to his Crystal Palace sermon in 1857. His Metropolitan Tabernacle church in Southwark held 6,000 worshippers.

Clearance and Famine

Many people from the Scottish Highlands emigrated after 1745. Some did so voluntarily, but others were forced out in 'the clearances'. In Ireland, mass emigration followed famines during the 1840s.

Leaving the Land

In Scotland, emigration was a constant factor in Highland life after 1750. Thousands of men were taken by the army to form new regiments for the French wars. Others left of their own free will after the bad harvests of the early 1760s, attracted by the abundance of better land in the colonies.

The Coming of Sheep

In the peace that followed the Battle of Culloden, Highland chiefs no longer needed warriors paying rent in military service. Instead these landowners wanted fine houses in Edinburgh and London, and for that they needed money. Wealthy southern sheep farmers were happy to pay cash to graze their flocks on Highland estates. In 1785, one grazing area in Glen Shiel was let for £310, more than thirty times what local farmers could pay. In 1826, the entire population of the island of Rum was evicted and replaced by one farmer with over 8,000 sheep.

As sheep farms were established across the Highlands, landowners evicted small-scale farmers from their homes and lands in a process called 'the clearances'. This painting shows a Highland chieftain and his family preparing to leave Scotland for good.

Strathnaver

The most brutal of the clearances occurred in Sutherland, where 15,000 small farmers were forcibly evicted to make way for sheep. The landowner, the Marquis of Stafford, wanted to improve his estates; he offered his tenants land on the coast where they could make a new living from fishing. However, in 1814 at Strathnaver Stafford's agents torched the houses and a woman burned to death. The resulting trial scandalized the nation and won public sympathy for the farmers. But the clearances continued, especially after 1850 when wealthy incomers from the south bought Highland estates and cleared them for deer and grouse shooting.

Around one million people in Ireland died of starvation when the potato crop failed for three years running.

Up to two million people emigrated from Ireland to seek a better life, many crossing the Atlantic to North America.

The Great Famine

Between 1800 and 1841, the population of Ireland doubled to eight-and-a-half million. Most of the Irish were farmers working small land-holdings. In 1845, the all-important Irish potato crop was infested with 'blight', an airborne fungus that turned the tubers into a foul-smelling mush. Three of the next four harvests were also blighted, leaving millions starving. The London government was slow to act and did too little to help. The winter of 1846-47 was especially cold and hit hard upon a weakened population. An estimated one million Irish people died between 1845 and 1849. Another two million migrated, many to Liverpool, Glasgow and South Wales, though others went to the United States and Canada. Large parts of rural Ireland were depopulated, and whole communities vanished.

King Potato

In Ireland, potatoes were the main crop because they were twice as nutritious as cereals. 'King Potato' was the staple food of around four million rural Irish. Such was the scale of poverty in Ireland, however, that many families only survived by doing seasonal work on the farms of Scotland and western England.

Votes for More People

After 1832, the right to vote was extended to a wider number of people. Some feared that this would spark revolution, but others saw it as a way to manage change.

A Rotten Parliament

Parliament remained unreformed until 1832. Though the British population had risen to twenty-four million, there were only 435,000 voters. Important landowners decided county elections, and many towns were rotten or pocket boroughs. Those few people with the right to vote expected to be bribed. Electors had to vote in public on a wooden stage or husting. This meant it was easy to threaten or persuade them to vote in a certain way.

Reform Crisis

In 1830, the industrial towns that produced much of the nation's wealth still had no representation in Parliament. Many respectable business people now wanted to be involved in the running of the country. In 1831, a new Whig government resolved to reform Parliament. However, in the House of Lords, Tories opposed to any change in the system defeated the first two Reform Bills that the Whigs introduced into Parliament. There were riots throughout Britain and public buildings were destroyed by mobs. A third Reform Bill finally passed into law in 1832, despite the reluctance of the king and the opposition of many in the House of Lords.

Open elections held at hustings were scenes of riotous disorder. Bribery and corruption took place there on a huge scale.

Moderate Reform

The 1832 Reform Act abolished the worst rotten boroughs, which were mostly in the south and south-west of England. Industrial towns in the north and midlands of England and in central Scotland were allowed to elect members of Parliament to the House of Commons, as were some London districts. An additional 217,000 people, mainly prosperous middle-class men, were given the right to vote. But the radicals and working people who had demonstrated for reform in the industrial cities were still unable to vote. Many felt betrayed by the Whigs and looked for other ways to press for change.

A Leap in the Dark

In the 1860s, Prime Minister Benjamin Disraeli hoped to strengthen the middle-class Conservative vote when he introduced his Reform Bill in 1867. By the time the bill was passed, however, it had been changed to include quite lowly town tradespeople. A million new voters were created, doubling the electorate, but most British adults still had no vote. Nevertheless, it was increasingly clear that the British public could be trusted to have a say in the choice of government without revolution breaking out in the streets.

Voting in Secret

In 1872, public voting on the hustings was replaced by secret ballot. This allowed electors to vote without fear of victimization. In 1884, a third Reform Act added another two million householders to the existing three million voters. Britain was not a full democracy, but many more people had a political stake in the country.

The First Reform Bill is finally passed by the House of Lords in 1832.

Timeline

1832	• First Reform Act does away with worst electoral abuses
1867	• Second Reform Act gives vote to all male householders
1872	• Ballot Act introduces secret voting and does away with the public hustings
1884	• Electorate increases to over five-and-a-half million people

Ireland

Laws against Catholics were designed to preserve the special privileges of Protestants. After 1790 however, Irish Catholics organized to fight for equality.

The eviction of poor tenant farmers by landlords who were often absent from Ireland built up resentment in the native Irish population.

Penal Laws

After 1691, Catholics were banned from the Dublin Parliament and from working as teachers or lawyers. It was made difficult for them to buy or inherit land and they were forbidden from owing firearms. The law was also used to control the Irish economy. Irish wool merchants and farmers were forced to sell their entire output to England, but at set prices that were usually poor.

Ireland and the French Revolution

Many Irish supported the ideas of the French revolutionaries. In 1792, the republican Wolfe Tone founded the Society of the United Irishmen to fight for the rights of all Irishmen. Tone died in an unsuccessful rebellion in 1798. However, London was forced to take more interest in Irish affairs and to unite the Dublin and British parliaments. The Dublin Parliament was abolished and, from 1801 onwards, one hundred Irish MPs sat in the London Parliament.

Emancipation

Daniel O'Connell preferred non-violent ways of bringing change to Ireland. His Catholic Association collected penny subscriptions for its campaign to abolish the laws against

Timeline

1828	• Daniel O'Connell elected to Parliament in Westminster but unable to take his seat
1829	• Wellington creates a Bill for Catholic Emancipation
1848	• Armed rebellion of Young Ireland fails at Ballingarry in County Tipperary
1867	• Fenian activities in England shock British public opinion
1886	• Liberal Party badly spilt over Irish Home Rule Bill
1893	• Gladstone's second Home Rule Bill defeated by the Lords

Catholics. Elected in 1828, the Catholic O'Connell was unable to take his seat in Parliament. Fearing another Irish rebellion, Prime Minister Wellington decided to give Catholics the vote, but only if they met high property qualifications. Wellington hoped this would ensure that Ireland returned moderate MPs to Parliament. However, Irish affairs turned more violent and groups of nationalists who wanted Irish freedom emerged. They included Young Ireland, who attempted an armed rebellion in 1848, and the Fenian Brotherhood, who carried out armed attacks on British gaols to free their imprisoned members.

Charles Stewart Parnell, founder of the Irish Parliamentary Party.

Parnell

By the 1880s, the Irish countryside was on the brink of revolution. Cheap American grain was flooding the market, forcing landowners to modernize their estates and evict their tenants. Many of these poor farmers took a violent revenge on their former landlords. The Irish Land League organized rent strikes and boycotts. Landowners who evicted their tenants were isolated by the local community and were unable to purchase goods and services. In Parliament, Charles Stewart Parnell formed the Irish Parliamentary Party. At the head of eighty 'nationalist' Irish MPs, Parnell aimed to obstruct all parliamentary legislation at Westminster until the problems of Ireland were solved.

The Irish Land League demonstrated against the forced evictions of tenants from their land.

Home Rule Bills

After 1885, Prime Minister William Gladstone needed support from the nationalists in the Commons. He introduced an Irish Home Rule Bill, which planned to devolve authority for all domestic issues to Dublin, reserving only defence and foreign policy at the London Parliament. The issue split the Liberals apart and the bill was defeated by thirty votes. Gladstone presented a second Home Rule Bill, but it was voted down in the Lords. The solution to Ireland's problems still seemed far away.

Imperial Adventures

In 1783, Britain lost its first empire in North America after a bitter war. However, new colonies in Africa and Asia restored Britain's position as the leading imperial power.

Revolutionary War

Most settlers in the American colonies felt they were British, but they resented being taxed by London without having representatives in Parliament. With every passing year, the colonists grew further apart from Britain. Fighting broke out in 1775. Britain's experienced army and navy expected to defeat the American rebels easily. But American General Washington skilfully kept his army together and American confidence grew. The French joined the American side in 1778, and by 1781 the British were besieged at Yorktown in Virginia by a much larger Franco-American force. In 1783, Britain accepted the independence of the United States of America.

American colonists raise the Stars and Stripes, the flag of the new United States of America.

India

In 1799, the British-run East India Company took control of the rich kingdom of Mysore. In 1816 the Gurkha warriors of Nepal became valuable allies to the British and, in 1819, the power of the Marathas chiefs of central India was broken. The ruling British now tried to eliminate the custom of *suttee* (the burning of widows on their husbands' funeral pyres) and the *tuggee* (a secret brotherhood of assassins). Modern roads and postal and telegraph systems were established while the first railway began in 1853. But the speed of these changes inspired Indian opposition.

Mutiny

In 1857, Indian troops refused to use rifle cartridges that had been greased with pig fat because touching this was against their religion. A group of mutineers killed their officers, marched on Delhi and proclaimed a Mogul prince as emperor. At Cawnpore, hundreds of

The fierce Gurkha warriors of mountainous Nepal resisted the British at first but then became their loyal allies.

British, including women and children, were massacred. In Lucknow, the British garrison was besieged for four months. The British took merciless revenge on the mutineers. After 1857, London took full control of India but the British there kept at a greater distance from the general population.

African Scramble

In Africa in 1800 Britain possessed a few former slaving posts on the River Gambia and on the Gold Coast. Sierra Leone became a colony in 1807 and the southern Cape became British after Napoleon's downfall. After 1875, Britain joined a 'scramble' by the main European powers to create empires in Africa. It had taken control of Nigeria, Kenya and Uganda by the 1890s.

African Wars

In southern Africa, the British became involved in several bloody wars. At Isandlwana in 1879 a thousand British troops were destroyed by the disciplined Zulu brigades. However, the Zulus' lack of firepower was exposed at Rorke's Drift, where a small number of Welsh troops held out against 4,000 warriors.

Boer leader Paul Kruger clashed with the British in Africa in the 1880s.

The Boers were farmers of Dutch origin who had settled in southern Africa. They twice fought Britain to keep their independence. They were only very slowly rounded up and defeated after Britain sent huge armies to South Africa between 1899 and 1902.

The Zulu chief Cetshwayo approaches British troops with a peace offering after his defeat at the Battle of Ulundi in 1879.

Timeline

1775	• American sharpshooters begin war against British
1776	• Americans declare independence from Britain
1778	• Americans win victory over British at Saratoga
1781	• British surrender at Yorktown
1799	• British forces win major victory in India
1816	• Gurkhas are defeated and British take control of Nepal
1819	• Marathas chiefs of central India are subdued
1848-56	• British modernize the infrastructure of India
1857-8	• Indian Mutiny shocks British
1858	• East India Company abolished and British government established
1875-1900	• European powers scramble for African colonies
1879	• Zulus finally defeated at Ulundi
1899	• Boer units invade Cape Colony and Natal
1902	• Boer War ends with peace of Vereeniging

Age of Improvement

The long reign of Queen Victoria saw many social improvements in Britain as a result of the spread of education and science.

Ragged Schools

In early Victorian England, secondary education was largely restricted to those few wealthy boys who went to public schools. Some poor children learned to read and write at 'ragged schools' run by charities. The Factory Acts of 1833 and 1844 forced employers to give their child workers daily schooling. However, most Victorian schools offered only a few subjects taught by untrained staff in cramped surroundings.

State Schools

The expansion of the electorate in 1867 underlined the need to ensure that the nation's citizens could read and vote wisely. In 1870, schooling was made compulsory in England while state school fees were abolished in 1890. Scotland already had many successful burgh and charitable schools. Numerous Scots, such as Dr Andrew Bell of Madras, had become well-known educational thinkers. In 1872 state schools were introduced in Scotland, finally bringing about the old Scottish Parliament's vision for a school in every parish.

Lasting sixty-four years, from 1837 to 1901, the reign of Queen Victoria was a period of immense social and technological change and improvement.

The Press

In 1841, one third of Britons could not read or write. By 1900, thanks to education and new print technologies, there were thirty-two daily newspapers in London alone, catering for all levels of society. Distribution by railways also helped national daily papers to build huge circulations. By 1890, the *Daily Telegraph* was read in over 300,000 homes around the country. The halfpenny *Daily Mail* appeared in 1896, undercutting its penny rivals. The *Mail*'s concentration on popular news meant that it soon established a daily readership of more than 500,000.

Lister's Spray

Standards of health care improved as medical knowledge increased. At St Thomas's Hospital in London, Florence Nightingale's school of nursing provided new levels of professional care. Stethoscopes were in common use by the 1850s and microscopes were beginning to make a contribution to medical research. In Glasgow, Joseph Lister developed an antiseptic carbolic spray in 1865 that helped defeat infections in patients following surgery.

Joseph Lister developed his carbolic spray to stop airborne infections from entering wounds.

Towards the Modern Age

By the end of the Victorian period, people who had learned to read by candlelight as children were witnessing a new age of electricity. In 1866, an undersea telegraph cable linked London to America and it was soon possible to send a message around the world. In 1876, Alexander Graham Bell perfected the telephone and the first London telephone exchange was set up three years later. In 1878, the chemist Joseph Swan demonstrated his patent electric lightbulb in Newcastle. Britain was being transformed by education and science. Victorians looked forward to the 20th century and imagined a future age of peace and progress.

Timeline

1833	• Factory Act forces mill owners to educate their child workers
1865-9	• Lister develops his principles of antiseptic care
1866	• First transatlantic telegraph cable from London to USA
1870s	• Establishment of state education system
1876	• Alexander Graham Bell demonstrates the telephone
1878	• Sunderland-born Joseph Swan makes the first electric light bulb
1896	• Appearance of the *Daily Mail*

Alexander Graham Bell was brought up in Scotland before emigrating to Canada. His studies in communicating sound electrically led to the invention of the telephone.

Glossary

adulterate to make a thing poorer in quality

aqueduct a bridge that carries a canal across a valley or river

ballot a vote

borough a town with some powers of self-government

boycott refuse to buy or handle goods

Cabinet group of government ministers closest to the Prime Minister

charismatic having great personal qualities such as energy and charm

civil service officials who run the government

coke a solid fuel derived from coal

colonist someone who goes to live in a colony (see below)

colony a territory owned by another country, usually for trading

Conservatives political party that developed out of the Tories in the 1860s

democratic when ordinary people have a say in choosing the government

devolve to pass power and authority to another institution

electorate all the people in a country with the right to vote in elections

emigrate to leave one's own country to settle permanently in another

Evangelical Christian ministers who spread the Gospel and did good works for society

evict to throw someone out of their home and/or off their land

fodder crops crops grown to feed cattle and sheep during the winter

hustings a platform on which voters had to declare their vote in public

justice of the peace a magistrate entrusted to keep order in England and Wales

laissez faire the belief that government should not interfere in social and business affairs

lease the legal agreement between a landowner and a tenant

legislation the laws of a country and the process of making them

missionary a person sent on a religious mission

nationalists Irish politicians who wanted more power for the Irish government

Penal Laws laws to limit the rights of Catholics in Ireland

radical in favour of social or political reform

reform to make the political system fairer and more democratic

relief help, such as money and accommodation, given to the very poor

repeal to reverse or abolish a law so that it no longer has any legal force

republican describes a state in which power is held by the people and their elected representatives, rather than a king or queen

sedition the charge of being treacherous and causing a rebellion

smelt to extract metal from ore by heating and melting

speculator a person who invests in business in the hope of vast or sudden financial gain

subsidy money given to someone, usually by government, to make up their wages

trade union an association of workers, formed to protect and further their rights

turnpike a bar to stop travellers from getting on to a road unless they pay

vaccination injecting small, safe amounts of an illness into someone to accustom their body to the disease

winding-wheel mechanism above a coalmine used to lower men and tools

workhouse an institution in which the very poor received food and a place to sleep in return for work

Timeline

1721-42	• Government by Robert Walpole, the first 'Prime Minister'
1740s	• Growth of Methodist movement
1756-63	• Britain wins control of North America and India
1780-1820	• Start of Highland clearances
1780-1850	• The great age of British industrial success and innovation
1783	• Britain loses the thirteen rebellious colonies of the USA
1785	• Construction of first mechanized power-looms
1793-1815	• Wars against Revolutionary and Napoleonic France
1801	• Union of British and Irish Parliaments
1805	• Royal Navy wins at Trafalgar
1815	• Final victory over Napoleon at Waterloo in Belgium
1819	• Massacre at 'Peterloo'
1829	• Propertied Roman Catholics given the right to vote
1830s	• First passenger railways
1833	• First Factory Act
1832	• Great Reform Act
1834	• Tolpuddle Martyrs arrested for swearing trade union oaths
1842	• Mines Act
1845-50	• Irish potato famines
1857	• Indian Mutiny shakes British imperial confidence
1867	• Second Reform Act
1870-72	• Education Acts set up state school systems in Britain
1872	• Voting becomes secret rather than done on public platforms
1879	• British forces eventually defeat the Zulu nation in South Africa
1884	• Third Reform Act
1899-1902	• Britain shocked by poor performance in the Second Boer War

Further Information

Books

History From Buildings: Victorian Britain, Tim Locke, Franklin Watts, 2006

Britain 1750–1900, John Clare, Hodder Murray, 2003

Britain in Victorian Times, Tim Locke, Franklin Watts, 2003

Victorians, History Snapshots, Sarah Ridley, Franklin Watts, 2007

Scotland 1700–1900, Richard Dargie, Heinemann, 2001

The Impact of Empire: Colonialism 1500–2000, Michael Riley, Hodder Murray, 2004

Websites

www.britainexpress.com/History/stuarts
clearly written introductions to main events such as the Corn Laws, Chartism and the Great Exhibition

www.parliament.uk/about/history.cfm
detailed description of key moments in Parliament's development in Georgian and Victorian times, such as the 1832 Reform Act

www.bbc.co.uk/history
illustrated accounts of important moments in the period 1700–1900, with timelines and links to other illustrated sites

www.learningcurve.gov.uk/victorianbritain/
well-illustrated investigations of issues in Victorian history on themes such as health, social improvement, industrial change, law and order and political agitation, with interactive games

www.cauldeenprimary.co.uk/victorian/index.htm
well-illustrated and informative website generated by pupils at Cauldeen Primary in Inverness

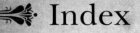

Index

*Numbers in **bold** refer to illustrations.*